A Choosing

Other titles by Liz Lochhead

A Choosing

The Selected Poems of Liz Lochhead

FOREWORD BY
CAROL ANN DUFFY

This edition first published in paperback in Great Britain in 2011 by
Polygon, an imprint of Birlinn Ltd

West Newington House
10 Newington Road
Edinburgh
EH9 1QS

www.polygonbooks.co.uk

ISBN 978 1 84697 207 2
eBook ISBN 978 0 85790 104 0

Reprinted in 2012

British Library Cataloguing-in-Publication Data
A catalogue record for this book is available on request
from the British Library

Typeset in Dante by Koinonia, Bury, Lancashire
ow

for Tom, always

Contents

Foreword

Liz Lochhead first appeared in print in 1972 with the award-winning publication *Memo for Spring*, and it is hard to say when a small pamphlet of poems has made such an impact. Lochhead's *Spring* blossomed out into the very male landscape of Scottish poetry and somehow managed to make that landscape female. Throughout her subsequent work, in poems such as 'What the Pool Said, on Midsummer's Day', Liz Lochhead has continued to find new ways through language of claiming her country. Her appointment as Makar in 2011, succeeding her dear friend Edwin Morgan, had a sense of rightness and inevitability about it. Her unique voice, a warm broth of quirky rhythms, streetwise speech patterns, showbiz pazzaz, tender lyricism and Scots, liberated a generation of women writers: Kathleen Jamie, Janice Galloway, Ali Smith, Jackie Kay and many more have all been influenced and inspired by her.

Lochhead's early work combined wit and poetry with a feminist aesthetic that felt fresh and exciting, and her work continues to display a zeitgeisty energy. Her monologues about ordinary women in trying or comic situations gained her a popularity which sees her today established as a National Treasure, and yet she remains essentially modest and humble – a modesty rooted in her skill and sensitivity as a love poet. The recent love poems which open this collection are among her finest work.

There's a famous painting by Sandy Moffat, *Poets' Pub* (1980) that depicts a literary world populated exclusively by men. It would be impossible to paint that picture today, because the faces of Scottish writers have changed forever, and much of that is due to Lochhead – a pioneer in her own country, a trailblazer. 'Poets need not be garlanded,' writes Liz Lochhead in the final poem here – but she *is* garlanded, justly so, and is well loved for her generous, life-enhancing poetry.

Carol Ann Duffy, June 2011

Author's Note

I don't want to say anything about the poems in this book except: here they are. (A boy in a school once said to me, 'See when you wrote that poem about the bull, what were you *really* trying to say?' – a question which both struck me dumb and made me sad for him; his teaching had made him feel that a poem was a coded way of saying something else. A tedious code, too, that he had to crack, and prove he'd cracked it in an essay, and pass an exam. 'Well, *that* really,' was all I could, eventually, manage.)

About this particular choosing (though another day, another year, I might have come out with a quite different selection, who knows?) – and, especially about the ordering of the poems, all I'll say is the obvious: that they aren't put together chronologically, but I've, instead, let one poem suggest a following sister poem that seems, to me at least, somehow to belong with it.

So that, for instance, a poem like 'The Choosing' – personal, autobiographical and one of the first things I ever wrote (about forty-five years ago in the late 1960s when I was eighteen) finds itself up against 'Kidspoem/Bairnsang', a 'first-the-phone-call' poem originally written on commission for a BBC London Education programme – sometime in the mid or late 1990s – as 'a dialect poem' with the worthy aim of encouraging school children from John O' Groats to Land's End to realise they had the right to keep writing, 'creatively' at least, in 'hometown English'. It was an occasional piece that I decided later was worth keeping – and worth promoting to 'poem' status.

See, I do write quite a lot of 'occasional' poems, light verse, rhyming – often rude-and-rhyming – poems, entertainments, out-loud performance pieces, dramatic monologues – and I'm certainly not ashamed of them at all. They are good fun (as well as sometimes, technically, quite hard work) to write, and, yes, audiences at poetry readings enjoy them. But in *A Choosing* you won't find the 'Vymura Shade Card' or 'Verena', just the ones which finally retain enough mystery for me to think of them as 'proper poems'.

It is painful going back over your own work, your own life, but, in the end, I quite enjoyed and became interested in making what seemed to me to be these new connections strung out over time, even if to others they might well appear to be just a lucky bag, a random flinging-together without much rhyme or reason.

It is a pleasure, though, to see the making of the book get to its final stages, to proof it, to work with others on choosing the cover. From among a few drawings of mine I've kept, charcoal or oil-pastel studies for long-lost canvases from my first year at Glasgow School of Art – drawings done at exactly the same time as I was writing the very earliest pieces in this book like 'The Choosing' – everyone seems to want to go with *Girl Undressing: black bra, red tights, pink shoes* from 1967. This feels like a nice emotional connection in 2011.

I'd like to thank, very much indeed, for their advice with the contents of this selection – I really could not have done it without them – Robyn Marsack of the Scottish Poetry Library, and Peggy Hughes of the same excellent organisation. And Sarah Ream – a brilliant editor from initial concept down to sensitive nit-picking proofing and copy-editing. And, as ever, my patient editor at Polygon, Neville Moir, and book-designer, book-lover, Jim Hutcheson – indeed to all at Polygon. Thanks to all these good friends.

And – above all – to Carol Ann Duffy, not just for her introduction here, but for her generosity, support, good advice, love and encouragement, which I depend on always, in my life as well as in my work.

Liz Lochhead
June 2011

A Choosing

A Night In

Darling, tonight I want to celebrate
not your birthday, no, nor mine.
It's not the anniversary of when we met,
first went to bed or got married, and the wine
is supermarket plonk. I'm just about to grate
rat-trap cheddar on the veggie bake that'll do us fine.

But it's far from the feast that – knowing you'll be soon,
and suddenly so glad to just be me and here,
now, in our bright kitchen – I wish I'd stopped and gone
and shopped for, planned and savoured earlier.
Come home! It's been a long day. Now the perfect moon
through our high windows rises round and clear.

Persimmons

(for Tom)

you must've
· loved
those three globes of gorgeous orange
dense and glowing in our winter kitchen
enough
to put coloured pencil and biro to the
reddest page left in your rainbow sketchbook
and make this drawing of
three persimmons in that Chinese bowl.

the supermarket flagged them up as
this season's sharon fruit
but we prefer *persimmon* (for
didn't it seem the rose of
their other name
would neither taste or sound as sweet,
would be a fruit of quite
another colour?)

such strange fruit . . . we bit and ate,
enjoyed.
before we did you drew them.
– oh, you'd say, so what?
(drawing, to you, is as everyday as apples)
but I know
they'd have come and gone like Christmas
if you'd not put them down
and made them worth more than the paper
they're inscribed on – see
those deft soft strokes of
aquamarine and white that
make our table-top lie flat, the fruits
plump out real and round and
perfectly persimmon-coloured .
upon their lilac shadows in the bowl's deep –

still life
still life, sweetheart,
in what's already eaten and done with.
now, looking, I can taste again.

Neckties

Paisleys squirm with spermatozoa.
All yang, no yin. Liberties are peacocks.
Old school types still hide behind their prison bars.
Red braces, jacquards, watermarked brocades
are the most fun a chap can have
in a sober suit.

You know about knots,
could tie, I bet, a bowtie properly
in the dark with your eyes shut, but
we've a diagram hung up
beside the mirror in our bedroom.
Left over right, et cetera . . .
The half or double Windsor,
even that extra fancy one it takes
an extra long tie to pull off successfully.
You know the times a simple schoolboy four-in-hand
will be what's wanted.

I didn't used to be married.
Once neckties were coiled occasional serpents
on the dressing-table by my bed
beside the car-keys and the teetering
temporary leaning towers of change.
They were dangerous nooses on the backs of chairs
or funny fishes in the debris on the floor.
I should have known better.

Picture me away from you
cruising the high streets
under the watchful eyes of shopboys
fingering their limp silks
wondering what would please you.
Watch out, someday I'll bring you back a naked lady,
a painted kipper, maybe a bootlace
dangling from a silver dollar
and matching collarpoints.

You could get away with anything
you're that goodlooking.
Did you like that screenprinted slimjim from Covent Garden?

Once I got a beauty in a Cancer Shop
and a sort of forties effort in Oxfam for a song.
Not bad for one dull town.
The dead man's gravy stain wasn't the size of sixpence
and you can hide it behind your crocodile tie pin.

Vow: The Simplest, Hardest and the Truest Thing

One: We live in love, so finally are come today
        (beyond the gladrags and the sweet bouquet
        beyond cake or ring or all this fuss)
        to this, the simplest and the truest thing for us.

Other: If you can say, my love – and hand on heart –
        I will love you until death do us part –

One: Hand on heart,
        I will love you till death do us part.

Other: Then look me in my eyes – and now!
        and here! – this kiss we kiss shall be our vow.

Epithalamium

for Joe and Annie Thomson

For Marriage, love and love alone's the argument.
Sweet ceremony, then hand-in-hand we go
Taking to our changed, still dangerous days, our complement.
We think we know ourselves, but all we know
Is: love surprises us. It's like when sunlight flings
A sudden shaft that lights up glamorous the rain
Across a Glasgow street – or when Botanic Spring's
First crisp, dry breath turns February air champagne.

Delight's infectious – your quotidian friends
Put on, with gladrag finery today, your joy,
Renew in themselves the right true ends
They won't let old griefs, old lives destroy.
When at our lover's feet our opened selves we've laid
We find ourselves, and all the world, remade.

View of Scotland/Love Poem

Down on her hands and knees
at ten at night on Hogmanay,
my mother still giving it elbowgrease
jiffywaxing the vinolay. (This is too
ordinary to be nostalgia.) On the kitchen table
a newly opened tin of sockeye salmon.
Though we do not expect anyone,
the slab of black bun,
petticoat-tails fanned out
on bone china.
'Last year it was very quiet . . .'

Mum's got her rollers in with waveset
and her well-pressed good dress
slack across the candlewick upstairs.
Nearly half-ten already and her not shifted!
If we're to even hope to prosper
this midnight must find us
how we would like to be.
A new view of Scotland
with a dangling calendar
is propped under last year's,
ready to take its place.

Darling, it's thirty years since
anybody was able to trick me,
December thirty-first, into
*'looking into a mirror to see a lassie
wi as minny heids as days in the year'* –
and two already since,
familiar strangers at a party,
we did not know that we were
the happiness we wished each other
when the Bells went, did we?

All over the city
off-licences pull down their shutters,
people make for where they want to be
to bring the new year in.
In highrises and tenements
sunburst clocks tick
on dusted mantelshelves.
Everyone puts on their best spread of plenty
(for to even hope to prosper
this midnight must find us
how we would like to be).
So there's a bottle of sickly liqueur
among the booze in the alcove,
golden crusts on steak pies
like quilts on a double bed.
And this is where we live.
There is no time like the
present for a kiss.

After the War

for Susanne Ehrhardt

After the war
was the dull country I was born in.
The night of Stafford Cripps's budget
My dad inhaled the blue haze of one last Capstan
then packed it in.
'You were just months old . . .'
The Berlin airlift.
ATS and REME badges
rattled in our button box.

Were they surprised that everything was different now?
Did it cheese them off that it was just the same,
stuck in one room upstairs at my grandma's
jammed against the bars of my cot
with one mended featherstitch jumper drying
among the nappies on the winterdykes,
the puffed and married maroon counterpane
reflected in the swinging mirror of the wardrobe?
Radio plays. Them loving one another
biting pillows
in the dark while I was sleeping.
All the unmarried uncles were restless,
champing at the bit
for New Zealand, The Black Country, Corby.
My aunties saved up for the New Look.

By International Refugee Year
we had a square green lawn and twelve-inch telly.

1953

All the Dads, like you, that spring
had put the effort in.
Stepped on it with brand new spades
to slice and turn
clay-heavy wet yellow earth
to clods that stank of clay
and were well marbled
with worms and rubble.
You set paths straight
with slabs it took two men to lift.
Tipped barrowloads of topsoil. Riddled.
Sowed grass seed from illustrated packets
that showed tall flowers, long English lawns
striped green like marrows. Then
stretched over paper bowties on strings
to frighten birds.
So gardens happened
where the earth had been one raw wound.

And behind whitened windows
the Mums were stippling walls
or treadling Singers as they
ran rivers of curtain material
through the eye of a needle and out again,
fit to hang by Coronation Day.
This was in rooms
that had emptinesses, possibilities,
still smelled of shaved wood
and drying plaster.

In no time at all
in a neat estate a long time later
I will watch in a dawn
through a crack in drawn curtains
this lawn, the late September borders,
mature roses
and the undertaker coming up the path
carrying a pint of milk.

Sorting Through

The moment she died, my mother's dance dresses
turned from the colours they really were
to the colours I imagine them to be.
I can feel the weight of bumptoed silver shoes
swinging from their anklestraps as she swaggers
up the path towards *her* dad, light-headed
from airman's kisses. Here, at what I'll have to learn
to call *my father's house*, yes every
ragbag scrap of duster prints her even more vivid
than an Ilford snapshot on some seafront
in a white cardigan and that exact frock.
Old lipsticks. Liquid stockings.
Labels like *Harella*, *Gor-ray*, *Berketex*.
As I manhandle whole outfits into binbags for Oxfam
every mote in my eye is a utility mark
and this is useful:
the sadness of dispossessed dresses,
the decency of good coats roundshouldered
in the darkness of wardrobes,
the gravitas of lapels,
the invisible danders of skin fizzing off from them
like all that life that will not neatly end.

Social History

My mother never
had sex with anyone else
except my father. A week before
her three-day leave to get married
my mother was examined by the Army Doctor
and pronounced *virgo intacta*
twenty-four years old and virgo intacta
an unusual thing in the ATS
an unusual thing in wartime
if you believe even half of what you read
in the social history books.
And the joke was I wasn't even sure
your Dad was going to make it. Rumour was
they were going to cancel all leave prior to D Day
so it was touch and go till the last minute . . .

The sex my mother could've had
but didn't
sounded fantastic. Clever Jewish boys
from the East End of London
whirled her round the dance floors
niftily slow foxtrotting her into corners
telling her the khaki matched her eyes.
A soldier in a darkened carriage on a slow train
wept on her shoulder when he told her
that he'd lost his brother in North Africa.
Two naval ratings on Margate pier
slipped a string of cultured pearls in her pocket
said 'Miss, we just found these on the beach
and you are so pretty we thought you ought to have them.'
She had a very close and very tender
friendship with a lovely, lovely gentle NCO
from the North of England who told her she was
the image of his girlfriend. An Italian
prisoner of war sketched her portrait and
her sister who had her eye on him
was quite put out.

She didn't care for Yanks but that didn't
stop them trying. A Free Frenchman
fell in love with her. A Polish Airforceman
proposed. Any Scotsmen she met
down there had lovely educated accents
and tended to be Top Brass.
She mixed with folk from All Over.
Which was the beauty of the services
and the best of the party that was wartime,
while the buzzbombs overhead didn't quite
cut out.
She was quite capable of downing her half of bitter
and rolling out the barrel with all the other girls
without ending up squiffy up against the wall
afterwards with her knickers down, unlike some.
When they all rolled back to barracks late,
swinging their lisle-stockinged legs
from the tailgate of a lorry, singing Appleblossom Time,
Military Policemen turned a blind eye
in exchange for nothing more than a smile.
Officers messed around with her in the blackout,
but then my mother told them
she was engaged to be married to my father
and they acted like the officers and gentle-
men they were and backed off sharpish, so
my mother never
had sex with anyone else
except my father, which was a source
of pride to her, being of her generation
as it would have been a source
of shame to me, being of mine.

Some Old Photographs

weather evocative as scent
the romance of dark stormclouds
in big skies over the low wide river
        of long shadows and longer shafts of light

of smoke
    fabulous film-noir stills of Central Station
of freezing fog silvering the chilled, stilled parks
    of the glamorous past
    where drops on a rainmate are sequins
    in the lamplight, in the black-and-white

your young, still-lovely mother laughs, the
hem of her sundress whipped up
by a wind on a beach before you were even born

all the Dads in hats
are making for Central at five past five
in the snow, in the rain, in the sudden *what-a-scorcher*,
in the smog, their
belted dark overcoats white-spattered by the starlings

starlings swarming
in that perfect and permanent cloud
above what was
never really this photograph
but always all the passing now
and noise and stink and smoky breath of George Square

wee boays, a duchess, bunting, there's a
big launch on the Clyde
and that boat is yet to sail

For my Grandmother Knitting

There is no need they say
but the needles still move
their rhythms in the working of your hands
as easily
as if your hands
were once again those sure and skilful hands
of the fisher-girl.

You are old now
and your grasp of things is not so good
but master of your moments then
deft and swift
you slit the still-ticking quick silver fish.
Hard work it was too
of necessity.

But now they say there is no need
as the needles move
in the working of your hands
once the hands of the bride
with the hand-span waist
once the hands of the miner's wife
who scrubbed his back
in a tin bath by the coal fire
once the hands of the mother
of six who made do and mended
scraped and slaved slapped sometimes
when necessary.

But now they say there is no need
the kids they say grandma
have too much already
more than they can wear
too many scarves and cardigans –
gran you do too much
there's no necessity . . .

At your window you wave
them goodbye Sunday.
With your painful hands
big on shrunken wrists.
Swollen-jointed. Red. Arthritic. Old.
But the needles still move
their rhythms in the working of your hands
easily
as if your hands remembered
of their own accord the pattern
as if your hands had forgotten
how to stop.

Poem for my Sister

My little sister likes to try my shoes,
to strut in them,
admire her spindle-thin twelve-year-old legs
in this season's styles.
She says they fit her perfectly,
but wobbles
on their high heels, they're
hard to balance.

I like to watch my little sister
playing hopscotch, admire the neat hops-and-skips of her,
their quick peck,
never-missing their mark, not
over-stepping the line.
She is competent at peever.

I try to warn my little sister
about unsuitable shoes,
point out my own distorted feet, the callouses,
odd patches of hard skin.
I should not like to see her
in my shoes.
I wish she could stay
sure footed,
                    sensibly shod.

My Mother's Suitors

have come to court me
have come to call oh
yes with their wonderful world
war two moustaches their long
stem roses their cultivated
accents (they're English aren't they
at very least they're
Educated-Scots).
They are absolutely
au fait with menu-French
they know the language of flowers
& oh they'd die
rather than send a dozen yellow
they always get them right & red.
Their handwriting on the florist's card
slants neither too much to the left or right.

They are good sorts.
They have the profile for it – note
the not too much nose
the plenty chin. The
stockings they bring have no strings
& their square
capable hands are forever
lifting your hair and gently
pushing your head away from them
to fumble endearingly at your nape
with the clasp of the pretty heirloom
little necklace they know their
grandmother would have wanted
you to have.
(never opals – they know
that pearls mean tears).

They have come to call & we'll all
go walking under the black sky's
droning big bombers
among the ratatat of ack-ack.
We'll go dancing & tonight
shall I wear the lilac, or the
scarlet, or the white?

Poppies

My father said she'd be fined
at best, jailed maybe, the lady
whose high heels shattered the silence.
I sat on his knee, we were listening
to the silence on the radio.
My mother tutted, oh that it was terrible,
as over our air
those sharp heeltaps struck steel, rang clear
as a burst of gunfire or a laugh
through those wired-up silent streets around the Cenotaph.
Respect.
Remembrance.
Surely when all was said
two minutes' silence in November
wasn't much to ask for, for the dead?
Poppies on the mantelpiece, the photograph
of a boy in a forage cap, the polished
walnut veneer of the wireless,
the buzzing in the ears and when
the silence ended the heldfire voice
of the commentator, who was shocked,
naturally, but not
wanting to make too much of it.
Why did she do it?
Was she taken sick – but that was no
excuse, on the radio it said,
couldn't you picture it?
how grown soldiers buttoned in their uniforms
keeled over, fell like flies
trying to keep up the silence.
Maybe it was looking at the khaki button eye
and the woundwire stem
of the redrag poppy
pinned in her proper lapel
that made the lady stick a bloody bunch of them
behind her ear
and clash those high heels across the square,
a dancer.

Lanarkshire Girls

Coming into Glasgow
in our red bus through those green fields. And
Summer annoyed us thrusting
leafy branches through the upstairs windows.
Like a boy with a stick through railings,
rattling us. We bent whole treetops
squeezing through and they rained down twigs, broken
bits of foliage, old blossom on the roof,
chucked hard wee balls of unripe fruit,
drumming us out of the country.

Then it was
shabby schemes, gospel halls, chapels, Orange halls,
doctors' surgeries, the crematorium, the zoo,
gap sites where August already frittered the stuffing out of
unpurpling fireweed and splintering thistles
till the blank blue sky was dot-dot-dotted
with whiskery asterisks.

Soon the coherent cliffs of Tollcross,
the many mansions of those lovely red and
blackened tenements. Our country bus sped
past the city stops, the women in their
slippers at the doors of dairies,
the proud pubs on every corner, accelerated
along the glamorous Gallowgate, juddered by
Reeta's gallus fashions and the
gorgeous dragons of Terry Tattoo Artist, till it
spilled us out, fourteen years old, dreaming ourselves up,
with holiday money burning a hole in our pockets
at the corner of Jamaica Street.

The Choosing

We were first equal Mary and I –
with same-coloured ribbons in mouse-coloured hair
and with equal shyness
we curtseyed to the lady councillor
for copies of Collins' Children's Classics.
First equal, equally proud.

Best friends too Mary and I –
a common bond in being cleverest (equal)
in our small school's small class.
I remember
the competition for top desk
or to read aloud the lesson
at school service.
And my terrible fear
of her superiority at sums.

I remember the housing scheme
where we both stayed.
The same houses, different homes,
where the choices were made.

I don't know exactly why they moved,
but anyway they went.
Something about a three-apartment
and a cheaper rent.
But from the top deck of the high-school bus
I'd glimpse among the others on the corner
Mary's father, mufflered, contrasting strangely
with the elegant greyhounds by his side.
He didn't believe in high-school education,
especially for girls,
or in forking out for uniforms.

Ten years later on a Saturday –
I am coming from the library –

sitting near me on the bus,
Mary
with a husband who is tall,
curly-haired, has eyes
for no one else but Mary.
Her arms are round the full-shaped vase
that is her body.
Oh, you can see where the attraction lies
in Mary's life –
not that I envy her, really.

And I am coming from the library
with my arms full of books.
I think of those prizes that were ours for the taking
and wonder when the choices got made
we don't remember making.

Kidspoem/Bairnsang

it wis January
and a gey dreich day
the first day Ah went to the school
so my Mum happed me up in ma
good navy-blue napp coat wi the rid tartan hood
birled a scarf aroon ma neck
pu'ed oan ma pixie an my pawkies
it wis that bitter
said *noo ye'll no starve*
gie'd me a wee kiss and a kid-oan skelp oan the bum
and sent me aff across the playground
tae the place Ah'd learn to say
it was January
and a really dismal day
the first day I went to school
so my mother wrapped me up in my
best navy-blue top coat with the red tartan hood
twirled a scarf around my neck
pulled on my bobble-hat and mittens
it was so bitterly cold
said *now you won't freeze to death*
gave me a little kiss and a pretend slap on the bottom
and sent me off across the playground
to the place I'd learn to forget to say
it wis January
and a gey dreich day
the first day Ah went to the school
so my Mum happed me up in ma
good navy-blue napp coat wi the rid tartan hood
birled a scarf aroon ma neck
pu'ed oan ma pixie an ma pawkies
it wis that bitter.

Oh saying it was one thing
but when it came to writing it
in black and white
the way it had to be said
was as if you were posh, grown-up, male, English and dead.

In the Dreamschool

you are never the teacher.
The history lesson
goes on for ever.

Yammering the always
wrong answer to the hardest question
you stand up in nothing but
a washed-in vest.

In the dreamschool nothing can be covered up.
Fleeced, yellowing
you never learn.

Teacher is bigeyed behind
awesome bifocals
and his teeth are green.
An offered apple will only tempt the snake
curled under his chalkstripe jacket. Loch-
gelly, forked-tongue, tawse.
Moonfaced mongols drag you towards
the terrible lavatories.

Sawdust soaks up sour mistakes.

The Teachers

they taught
that what you wrote in ink
carried more weight than what you wrote in pencil
and could not be rubbed out.
Punctuation was difficult. Wars
were bad but sometimes necessary
in the face of absolute evil as they knew only too well.
Miss Prentice wore her poppy the whole month of November.
Miss Mathieson hit the loud pedal
on the piano and made us sing
The Flowers of the Forest.
Miss Ferguson deplored the Chinese custom
of footbinding but extolled the ingenuity
of terracing the paddyfields.
Someone she'd once known
had given her a kimono and a parasol.

Miss Prentice said the Empire had enlightened people
and been a two-way thing.
The Dutch grew bulbs and were our allies in
wooden shoes.

We grew bulbs on the window sills
beside the frogspawn that quickened into wriggling
commas or stayed full stop.
Some people in our class were stupid, full stop.
The leather tawse was coiled around the sweetie tin
in her desk beside the box of coloured blackboard chalk
Miss Ferguson never used.

Miss Prentice wore utility smocks.
Miss Mathieson had a moustache.
If your four-needled knitting got no
further than the heel you couldn't turn
then she'd keep you at your helio sewing
till its wobbling cross-stitch was specked with rusty blood.

Spelling hard words was easy when you knew how.

After a Warrant Sale

I watched her go,
Ann-next-door
(dry-eyed,
as dignified
as could be expected)
the day after they came,
sheriff court men
with the politeness of strangers
impersonally
to rip her home apart –
to tear her life along the dotted line
officially.

On the sideboard that went for fifteen bob,
a photograph.
Wedding-day Walter and
Ann: her hair was lightened,
and her heart, with hopes.
No one really knows
when it began to show –
trouble, dark roots.

It was common knowledge
there were faults on both sides,
and the blame –
whether it was over drink
or debt no one seems to know,
or what was owing to exactly whom.
Just in the end the warrant sale
and Ann's leaving.

But what seemed strange:
I wondered why,
having stayed long past the death of love
and the ashes of hope,
why pack it up and go
over some sticks of furniture

and the loss of one's only partially
paid-for washing machine?

Those who are older tell me,
after a married year or two
the comforts start to matter
more than the comforting.
But I am very young,
expecting not too much of love –
just that it should completely solve me.
And I can't understand.

Fragmentary

Twilight (six o'clock and
undrawn curtains). It's as if
                        upstairs
                              from me
lives some crazy projectionist
running all his reels at once.
Pub-sign neon scrawls credits on the sky that's
cinemascope for him. He
treats me to so many
simultaneous
home movies, situation comedies, kitchen-sink dramas
I can't make sense of them –
just snippets, snatches with the sound gone,
mouthings in a goldfish bowl.

The Offering

Never in a month of them
would you go back.
Sunday,
the late smell of bacon
then the hard small feeling
of the offering in the mitten.
Remember how the hat-elastic cut.
Oh the boredom,
and how a lick of spittle got purple dye or pink
from the hymn-book you worried.
Maybe your neighbour would
have technicoloured pictures of
Jesus curing lepers
between the frail tissue pages of her bible
or she'd stroke you with the velvet
of a pressed rosepetal
till someone sucking peppermint
and smelling of mothball
poked you and hissed that you weren't to fidget.
Remember the singing
(with words and actions)
and how you never quite
understood the one about Nic-
odemus Coming to the Lord by Night.

Sunday,
perhaps an auntie
would visit with a cousin.
Everyone would eat ice cream
and your mothers would compare you,
they'd stand you by the doorstop
and measure you up.

Sunday, maybe later in the evening
There'd be a Brethren Meeting.
Plain women wearing hats to cover
uncut hair. And

singing, under lamp-posts, out in our street!
And the leader
shouted the odds on Armageddon, he
tried to sell Salvation.
Everybody turned their televisions up.

Never in a month of them
should you go back.
Fond hope.
You'll still find you do not measure up.
The evangelist still mouths behind glass unheard.
You'll still not understand
the singing, the action or the word.
Ice cream will cloy, too sweet, too bland.
And the offering
still hard and knotted in your hand.

Obituary

We two in W2
walking,
and all the W2 ladies, their
hair coiffed and corrugated come
with well-done faces
from the hairdressers.
We together
laughing,
in our snobbery of lovers,
at their narrow vowels
and strange permed poodles.
Locked too long in love, our eyes
were unaccustomed to the commonplace.
          Seems silly now really.

We two in W2
walking
down Byres Road
passing unconcerned
a whole florist's
full of funerals,
the nightmare butcher's shop's
unnumbered horrors,
the hung fowls
and the cold fish
dead on the slab.
We saw ourselves duplicated
by the dozen in the chainstore
with no crisis of identity.
Headlines on newsagent's placards
caused us no alarm
Sandwichman's prophecies of doom
just slid off our backs.
The television showroom's window
showed us cities burning
in black and white but we

had no flicker of interest.
An ambulance charged screaming past
but all we noticed was the funny old
Saturday street musician.
   Seems silly now really.

We two one Sunday
at the art galleries
looking only at each other.
We two one Sunday
in the museum –
wondering why the ownership of a famous man
should make a simple object a museum piece –
and I afraid
to tell you how
sometimes I did not wash your coffee cup for days
or touched the books you lent me
when I did not want to read.
Well, even at the time
   that seemed a bit silly really.

Christmas found me
with other fond and foolish girls
at the menswear counters
shopping for the ties that bind.
March found me
guilty of too much hope.
   seems silly now really.

Poem for Other Poor Fools

Since you went I've only cried twice.
Oh never over you. Once
it was an old head at a bus window
and a waving hand.
Someone's granny, a careful clutcher of her handbag
and wearing a rainhat despite the fact
it wasn't raining. Yet
waving, waving to grandchildren already turned away
engrossed in sweets she had left them.
Old head. Waving hand.

> Oh she wasn't the type to expose herself
> to the vagaries of weather
> (a rainhat in no rain)
> yet waving, waving to those who had already
>   turned away.

Then once it was a beggar by the pub doorway
and his naked foot.
Some drunk old tramp,
player of an out-of-tune mouthorgan
and begging. Instead of his cap,
his boot for alms.
His playing was hopeless,
his foot bare in the gutter in the rain,
his big boot before him, empty, begging.
Oh it was a scream. I laughed
and laughed till I cried.

> It was just his poor
> pink and purple naked foot
>
>   out on a limb
>
> exposed.
> And how (his empty boot) he got nothing
>   in return.

Inventory

you left me
           nothing but nail
           parings orange peel
           empty nutshells half filled
           ashtrays dirty
           cups with dregs of
           nightcaps an odd hair
           or two of yours on my
           comb gap toothed
           bookshelves and a
           you shaped
           depression in my pillow.

Revelation

I remember once being shown the black bull
when a child at the farm for eggs and milk.
They called him Bob – as though perhaps
you could reduce a monster
with the charm of a friendly name.
At the threshold of his outhouse, someone
held my hand and let me peer inside.
At first, only black
and the hot reek of him. Then he was immense,
his edges merging with the darkness, just
a big bulk and a roar to be really scared of,
a trampling, and a clanking tense with the chain's jerk.
His eyes swivelled in the great wedge of his tossed head.
He roared his rage. His nostrils gaped like wounds.

And in the yard outside,
oblivious hens just picked their way about.
The faint and rather festive jingling
behind the mellow stone and hasp was all they knew
of that Black Mass, straining at his chains.
I had always half-known he existed –
this antidote and Anti-Christ, his anarchy
threatening the eggs, well rounded, self-contained –
and the placidity of milk.

I ran, my pigtails thumping on my back in fear,
past the big boys in the farm lane
who pulled the wings from butterflies and
blew up frogs with straws.
Past thorned hedge and harried nest,
scared of the eggs shattering –
only my small and shaking hand on the jug's rim
in case the milk should spill.

An Abortion

The first inkling I had of the beast's agony
was the something not right
of her scrabbling, scrabbling
to still not quite find
all four feet.
Sunk again, her cow-tongue lolled
then spiked the sky, she rolled
great gape-mouth, neck distended
in a Guernica of distress.
That got through to me all right
behind glass as I was
a whole flat field away.
It took an emblem-bellow
to drag me from my labour
at the barbed words on my desk top.

Close to, green foam flecked her muzzle
and drizzled between the big bared brown teeth.
Spasms, strong, primeval
as the pulsing locomotion of some
terrible underwater creature,
rippled down her flank
and her groan was the more awesome
for being drier, no louder than a cough.
When she tried to rise again
I saw it.
Membrane wrapped, the head of a calf
hung out and the wrong-looking bundle
of a knuckle. Then her rope-tail dropped
and she fell back on it, steamrollering it
under her.

When the summoned men came,
buttoning blue coveralls over
the Sunday lunches and good-suit waistcoats,
the wound string around one man's knuckles

meant business and the
curt thank-you-very-much of the other
dismissed me.

Shamed voyeur, back at my notebooks again
my peeled eyes caught the quick hoick
of the string loop, the dead thing flopping
to the grass, the cow on her knees and
up again, the men leaving, one
laughing at some punchline.

The thing is this. Left alone,
that cow licking at those lollop limbs
which had not formed properly
with her long tongue,
that strong tongue
which is a match for thistles
and salt-lick coarse as pumice stone
tenderly over and over again at
what has come out of her and she is responsible for
as if she cannot believe it will not
come alive,
not if she licks long enough.

Outside she is still licking, licking
till in the blue dusk
the men in blue come back again
and she turns, goes quietly with them
as if they were policemen
and she knew exactly what she were guilty of.

Notes on the Inadequacy of a Sketch

at Millport Cathedral, March 1970

Fields strung out so, piece-
meal on a crude felt-tip line,
in real life revealed ribs
where the plough had skinned them alive.
My scrawl took the edge off the dyke.
Sure. But omitted to mark how
it held together, the gravity
of the situation (it being
a huddle of rough stone forms in a cold climate)
how it was set to hump across hills, or at what
intervals over which stones exactly
snails had scribbled silver.
I jotted down how fence
squared up to dyke (but nothing of
the wool tufts caught on random barbs)
how it bordered on that
ridiculous scrap of grass
(but failed to record its precise
and peculiarly Scottish green).
I made a sheer facade
of the cruciform cathedral, stated
only that the rectory garden
slanted towards an empty greenhouse
on the graveyard's edge.
For gravestones, I set mere slabs right-
angling to a surface I took at face value.
(I did not explain how at my feet
sprawled a rickle of rabbit bones
ribcage and spine in splinters,
skull intact.) I probed no roots.
I did not trace either gravestones'
legends or their moss (it let me read
between the lines the stones' survivals).
I selected what seemed to be essentials.
Here, where wind and rain

made a scapegoat of a scarecrow, my pen
took it for an easy symbol. But it's plain
setting down in black and white
wasn't enough, nor underlining
certain subtleties. This sketch became
a simile at best. It's no metaphor.
It says *under prevailing conditions*
smoke from a damp bonfire was
equal in tonal value to the sea.
So what?
       Today on the empty
summer's sand the March rain needled no one.
(My sketch mentions no rain
neither how wet it was nor how straight
it fell nor that seagulls tried to call a halt
to it.) From my quick calligraphy of trees
no real loud rooks catcall the sea's
cold summersault.

Laundrette

We sit nebulous in steam.
It calms the air and makes the windows stream,
rippling the hinterland's big houses to a blur
of bedsits – not a patch on what they were before.

We stuff the tub, jam money in the slot,
sit back on rickle chairs
not reading. The paperbacks in our pockets curl.
Our eyes are riveted. Our own colours whirl.

We pour in smithereens of soap. The machine sobs
through its cycle. The rhythm throbs
and changes. Suds drool and slobber in the churn.
Our duds don't know which way to turn.

The dark shoves one man in,
lugging a bundle like a wandering Jew. Linen
washed in public here.
We let out of the bag who we are.

This young wife has a fine stack of sheets, each pair
a present. She admires their clean cut air
of colour-schemes and being chosen. Are the dyes fast?
This christening lather will be the first test.

This woman is deadpan before the rinse and sluice
of the family in a bagwash. Let them stew in their juice
to a final fankle, twisted, wrung out into rope,
hard to unravel. She sees a kaleidoscope

for her to narrow her eyes and blow smoke at, his overalls
and pants ballooning, tangling with her smalls
and the teeshirts skinned from her wriggling son.
She has a weather eye for what might shrink or run.

This dour man does for himself. Before him,
half lost, his small possessions swim.
Cast off, random
they nose and nudge the porthole glass like flotsam.

The Bargain

The river in January is fast and high.
You and I
are off to the Barrows.
Gathering police-horses twitch and fret
at the Tron end of London Road and Gallowgate.
The early kick-off we forgot
has us, three thirty, rubbing the wrong way
against all the ugly losers
getting ready to let fly
where the two rivers meet.

January, and we're
looking back, looking forward,
don't know which way

but the boy
with three beautiful Bakelite
Bush radios for sale in Meadow's Minimarket is
buttonpopping stationhopping he
doesn't miss a beat   sings along   it's easy
to every changing tune

Yes today we're in love aren't we?
with the whole splintering city
its big quick river   wintry bridges
its brazen black Victorian heart.
So what if every other tenement
wears its hearth on its gable end?
All I want
is my glad eye to catch
a glint in your flinty Northern face again
just once. Oh I know it's cold
and coming down
and no we never lingered long among
the Shipbank traders.
Paddy's Market   underneath the arches
stank too much today

the usual wetdog reek rising
from piles of old damp clothes.

Somebody absolutely steamboats he says on
sweet warm wine
swigged plaincover from a paper bag
squats in a puddle with nothing to sell
but three bent forks   a torn
calendar (last year's)
and a broken plastic sandal.
So we hadn't the stomach for it today.
We don't deserve a bargain then!
No connoisseur can afford to be too scrupulous
about keeping his hands clean.
There was no doubt   the rare   the beautiful
and the bugle-beaded   the real antique   dirt cheap
among the rags and drunks
you could easily take to the cleaners.

At the Barrows everything has its price
no haggling   believe me
this boy knows his radios.
Pure Utility
and what that's worth these days.
Suddenly the fifties are fashionable
and anything within a decade of art deco
a rarity you'll pay through the nose for.
The man with the patter and all these curtain lengths
in fibreglass is flabbergasted at the bargain
and says so in so many words.
Jesus, every other
arcade around here's
a 'Fire Surround Boutique' –
and we watch the struggling families –
father carrying hearth home
mother wound up with kids.
All the couples we know fall apart
or have kids.

Oh we've never shouldered much.
We'll stick to small ikons for our home –
as long as they're portable –
a dartboard   a peacock feather
a stucco photoframe.

We queue in a blue haze of hot fat
for Danny's Do-Nuts that grit
our teeth with granules of sugar
I keep
losing you and finding you –
two stalls away you thumb
through a complete set of manuals for
primary teachers in the thirties
I rub my sleeve
on a dusty Chinese saucer
till the gilt shows through.
Oh come on   we promised
we'd not let our affection for the slightly cracked
trap us into such expenditure again.
Oh even if it is a bargain
we won't buy.
The stallholder says we'll be the death of her
she says   see January
it's been the doldrums the day.

And it's packing-up time
with the dark coming early
and as cold as the river.
By the bus stop I show you
the beady bag and the maybe rosewood box
with the inlaid butterfly and the broken catch.
You've bought a record by the Shangri-las
a pin-stripe waistcoat that needs a stitch
it just won't get   and a book called *Enquire
Within – Upon Everything*.

The raw cold gets colder.
There doesn't seem to be a lot to say.
I wish we could either mend things
or learn to throw them away.

5th April 1990

for Edwin Morgan on his 70th birthday

Today I got back from Berlin and the broken Wall.
With bits of it.
Smithereens of history, the brittle confetti
of chiselled-off graffiti,
trickle on to the brave blue dogeared cover
of my signed copy of *Sonnets from Scotland*
that I had with me and have just unpacked.
It hasn't travelled well, but crumbled,
this souvenir I brought for fünfzig Pfennige,
picked out from the brightest chips,
from the priciest slabs with names
or obscenities half intact – all on offer
from that grinning gap-toothed Kreuzberg
Gastarbeiter kid who really thought
he had it made.
Well, he saw me coming all right –
another dumbcluck tourist
taking the slow curve of the Wall
towards Mariannenplatz, gawping at
the Bethanien-House artists mending
still-serviceable slogans on what was left standing.
This was a facelift the
chinking chisels of stonepeckers would
only worry at in turn and yet
they painted, and lovingly,
as if these fluorescents and enamels
would last one thousand years
and make good sense.

Every night I spent at Wannsee
at the Writers' House by the Lake,
Morgan's poems whirled me from space
to the bedrock of my own small
and multitudinous country, swung me
through centuries, ages, shifting geologies

till I was dizzy and dreamed
I was in the sands of the desert and the dead
as the poets lived it, just before my time,
then I was following Gerard Manley Hopkins
in priestly black up North Woodside Road
like a taunting Irish boy till I was suddenly,
stone-cold sober, contemplating De Quincey
out of his mind in Rottenrow.

And all there was was
the symmetry of these turning pages,
fourteen lines mirroring fourteen lines,
the small circle of light
from the Bauhaus lamp on my borrowed desk
and the sough of trees in the Grünewald.
And outside there was Berlin.
The moneychangers at Zoostation
fanning out fistfuls of Ostmarks,
little lozenges of polystyrene, drifts and
spills from the packaging of dragged
video recorders and ghetto blasters,
blown white as hailstones and as light as popcorn
about their feet.

There was the wasted acreage of the Polish market
beside the Nationalgalerie where
the Ein' Mark, Ein' Mark, Ein' Mark
everything cost was so slow coming in
some of these sellers-in-hell bought
bottles of berry vodka from fellow blackmarketeers
with all they'd made and more, gave up,
got too blitzed to even pretend
to peddle bits of tractor, tools, laces,
mushrooms from polluted fields
bashed tins filched from hungry Warsaw,
bumpy Eastern European school shoes
to the haggling Turkish families from
the U-bahn's Istanbul Express.

And now I'm home
with three painted Polish Easter eggs,
Hungarian opera duets, Romanian symphonies,
an uncopyrighted East German Mickey Mouse
painted the wrong colours,
funny-tasting chocolate
and the Rolling Stones 'in ctepeo'
Made in Bulgaria *Made in the Shade*.
And bits of the wall that are almost powder.
I think who could make sense of it?
Morgan could, yes Eddie could, he would.
And that makes me want to try.

Hafiz on Danforth Avenue

There are no nightingales in this lunchroom, but
I have all these presents wrapped in that cheap
Christmas paper printed with those cardinals
you said sang out too loud.
Waiting for the
last of the breakfast specials I fish out
from the bottom of my handbag your father's
copy of Hafiz you lent me. Old ink
on the flyleaf, the name
that is also your name, the date
and where he bought it.

No place
for a lady here at eleven a.m.
in bitter mid December on the Danforth – all these
Greek men at the counter
on their rooted stools, sallow
under astrakhan, brindled moustaches,
the clack of worrybeads, I catch
a flash of amber and tassels.
A toothpick, a gold filling –
'Tonight I gonna finish one gallon of wine.
Tony makes it great. Forget
the mortgages, the pressure, tonight
if my wife she drives me I can get loaded.'

'A laughing winecup, a tangle
of knotted hair' I tingle
remembering us side by side – I am reading
your old Hafiz, you the New Divan I
brought with me, somehow linking
Glasgow to Toronto to Teheran.
Later you stretch out,
the book is closed on the carpet,
a spiral of tangerine peel on the cover.

In the photograph you showed me Sunday
you are twelve, it is the year
you lived in Baghdad, you
are jug-eared, a proper cropped
North American boy.
There are two Iraqi taxidrivers,
a big Yankee car with
dangling charms of Islam. I can
smell the heat and the petrol.

'The morning breeze is the messenger of Love . . .
The beloved
is sometimes the seller of sweetmeats,
the poet an eloquent sugarloving parrot.'
And today's snowflakes
muffle the mounds of Best Canadian
pumpkins and hubbardsquash outside
next door's greengrocery.
Here, through chromium and steam
the sugar dredger, a plate of lemons,
jellies, sherbert-coloured wedges
of chiffon pie.

The beautiful black waitress
wears a white beanie.

They've written Merry Christmas with glitterdust
on the mirror here in Motorama
beside the poster which says
Cold, Beautiful
Milk.
The young lovers
holding hands under the next table
play on the jukebox
'You don't bring me flowers.'

And to tell you this is easy,
scribbling this was as simple

as the shopping-list it jostles
on the next page of my notebook.
Love, as well as bread and coffee
it says eggplants, olive oil
don't forget
the nutmeg and cinnamon.

Fourth of July Fireworks

The guests are gathered.
Boston-Irish Nancy, half in huff,
says, 'Better help yourselves,
you all know Mister's timing well enough.'
Aside at me she mutters,
'Millionaires can afford to let things wait.
Honest-to-God Mister would be late
for his own funeral.' Cigarstore Indian,
I hide behind my apron, wait and drink in all I can.

(We don't exist. They pick our trays,
Tom Collinses, Martinis and canapés.)

Oh horror, New England night,
when I fetched the ice down and that snake
looped my feet in the kitchen garden! I still shake.
'Harmless,' says Nancy.
I hear her hiss, 'Some host!
That beggar'll only get here when he's sure he's last.'

Fourth of July. Cape Cod. Dead on cue,
last-man Mister comes running to his barbecue.
Arms flailing like a cricketer's across the lawn
from his *'so English'* house with a flame red shirt on.

It's the cocktail hour. The air is still.
Mister gets busy on the charcoal grill.
Social-kissing women, backslapping men
has failed to break the ice. But then
Missiz appears like magic from the dusk.
Cool, ten years his junior, she smells of musk
and Madame Rochas. Two small spots of anger
high on her cheekbones linger.

When Mister says it's done enough
the guests spread ketchup on the fatted calf.
The night hots up. Liquor flows. Listless
couples come alive. A bit apart, restless,

Missiz sways gently on her own
to Glen Miller on the gramophone.
All eyes are on the soignée cling
of this year's leisure favourite, velvety stretch towelling
for patio-party wear. Those purples and electric pinks
'Just far too hectic altogether,' Nancy thinks.

(Ten years with Missiz, Nancy's face
is quite professional, impervious.)

Ice melts in the Martini tray. Midges
drown. The whole night edges
to a thunderstorm. Maybugs big as golfballs thud
as screendoors bounce them. But, after our blood,
divebombing mosquitoes dodge the mesh and slide
in down their own thin whine.
They bite despite insecticide.

All at sea,
white and dayglo orange fins spinnaker the bay.
Music blares
from the jazzed-up clubhouse round the Cape, Cotuit way.
The whole damn town is two thirds empty after Labour Day.
These summer people
migrate to Florida, lock, stock and barrel.
Tonight their parked cars sprawl the drive and trail
behind those his-and-hers coupled custom Cadillacs
like a comet tail.

(Oh I can see it all quite clearly, feeling small
and stone-cold sober. But I do not count at all.)

Out on the lawn the sprinklers, oddly luminous,
sputter like Roman Candles, ominous
as the sudden snap of queer clear light
from one weird streak unzips the dark.
The German Shepherd guard dogs bark.
A wind gets up. These beach-house boards
are flimsier than playing cards.

(Over the bay, like flares
odd rockets go up with a shock of stars.)

Mister drags off his box of fireworks to the shore.
Missiz drains her drink and hits the floor
with someone half her age. His snake-arms slur
around her waist. Eyes glaze. Sentence endings blur.
Missiz ('mutton dressed as lamb')
comes in slowly as the false-calm
lead-slow sea that slicks the beach. Sinatra sings.
The tide ravels up slowly, shelving things.

Raindrops big as bullets dent the roof we all stand under,
watching Canute's fireworks out-rage the storm,
try to steal its thunder.

Ontario October Going West

The wilderness tells the eye you won't
get very far with me says
tangle scribble says
pawmark and leafprint stippling layer on layer
says fernstitch herring-
bone   rusted wirewool to lie on   whisk-ear
blackthorn.
says strewn silky pillowstuffing   burst
milkweed.   says nudging
blunt bullrushes   (brown velvet)   fishhooked burr
bramble barb   vast feathery colourlessness.

The trees scream jaundice
canary   orange peel   adultery
oxblood   magenta.
the single drowned birch shrieks
fingerbone.
the lake says frankly this is
a very old trick   it's all
done with mirrors.

The barn (*see my*
ancient white hex sign in a circle) says
I'm twice as big and
beautiful as any house.
Winters like these   believe me
I have to be.

The railway says east west.

The prairie   when you get to it
says keep going.

The Empty Song

Today saw the last of my Spanish shampoo.
Lasted an age now that sharing with you,
such a thing of the past is.
Giant Size. The brand
was always a compromise.
My new one's tailored exactly to my needs.
Nonspill. Protein-rich.
Feeds body, promises to solve my problem hair.
Sweetheart, these days it's hard to care,
But oh oh insomniac moonlight
how unhoneyed is my middle of the night.
I could see you
far enough. Beyond me
how we'll get back together.
Campsites in Spain, moonlight,
heavy weather.

Today saw the end of my Spanish shampoo,
the end of my third month without you.

Noises in the Dark

The four a.m. call to the faithful wakes us,
its three-times off-key harmony of drones and wails.
Above our heads I snap the lightcord but the power fails
as usual leaving us in the dark. Tomorrow takes us
who knows where. What ruins? What towns? What smells?
Nothing shakes us.
We touch and today's too painful sunburn sticks and sears
apart again. Faithful to something three long years,
no fear, no final foreign dark quite breaks us.

Hotel habitués,
the ritually faithful wash their feet. Old plumbing grumbles.
The tap-leak in our rust-ringed basin tickles
irritant, incessant, an itch out of the dark. Whitewash crumbles
from the wall where the brittle cockroach trickles.
Fretful, faithful, wide to the dark, can we ever forget
this shabby town hotel, the shadow of the minaret?
Human or bird or animal? What was it cried?
The dark smear across the wall still unidentified.

My Rival's House

is peopled with many surfaces.
Ormolu and gilt, slipper satin,
lush velvet couches,
cushions so stiff you can't sink in.
Tables polished clear enough to see distortions in.

We take our shoes off at her door,
shuffle stocking-soled, tiptoe – the parquet floor
is beautiful and its surface must
be protected. Dust-
cover, drawn shade,
won't let the surface colour fade.

Silver sugar-tongs and silver salver,
my rival serves us tea.
She glosses over him and me.
I am all edges, a surface, a shell
and yet my rival thinks she means me well.
But what squirms beneath her surface I can tell.
Soon, my rival
capped tooth, polished nail
will fight, fight foul for her survival.
Deferential, daughterly, I sip
and thank her nicely for each bitter cup.

And I have much to thank her for.
This son she bore –
first blood to her –
never, never can escape scot free
the sour potluck of family.
And oh how close
this family that furnishes my rival's place.

Lady of the house.
Queen bee.
She is far more unconscious,
far more dangerous than me.

Listen, I was always my own worst enemy.
She has taken even this from me.

She dishes up her dreams for breakfast.
Dinner, and her salt tears pepper our soup.
She won't
give up.

Midsummer Night

Was that a donkey braying in my dream?
Couldn't make head or tail of it but
it hawhawed itself blue in the face
whatever it was. Still, confusion's clearly
what's called for in any comedy worth worrying about.
That and chance
which certainly seems to be
playing its part all right.
So we're laughing?
Get us, half enchanted and undecided
whether or not to give in to it,
wandering the wide woods on such a night like
the wrong pair of ill-met demi-
lovers we most likely are
in far too high a pollen count for
anybody's comfort. This is the
silly season though – you said so yourself –
surely a solstice is a time for going to extremes.
Have a heart, though, I've always been
the equinox sort – white nights
and talking till birdsong
are as new a taste to me as the
piney retsina we sat late in the restaurant with,
till one. And still no real dark yet
to go home in.

Earlier, between
the World Cup and Wimbledon the blue
TV lights flickered from every douce house
in the solid suburbs we drove through to come
to such a shifting place.
Remember the horses
how silently they moved
from dark woods.
'Would you call this a green glade?' you
asking gravely with a glint,

the lilac haze and three rooks on the long meadow,
that russet shape that changed
we could swear it, and stretched
and lengthened to a fox and back to prick-eared
hare again. Nothing tonight could decide
what form to take.

We are good and strange to one another and no mistake.

What the Pool Said, on Midsummer's Day

I've led you by my garrulous banks, babbling
on and on till – drunk on air
and sure it's only water talking –
you come at last to my silence.
Listen, I'm dark
and still and deep enough.
Even this hottest gonging sun
on this longest day
can't white me out.
What are you waiting for?
I lie here, inviting, winking you in.

The woman was easy.
Like to like, I called her, she came.
In no time I had her
out of herself, slipping on my water-stockings,
leaning into, being cupped and clasped
in my green glass bra.
But it's you I want, and you know it, man.
I watch you, stripped, knee-deep
in my shallows, telling yourself
that what makes you gasp
and balls your gut
is not my coldness but your own fear.

– Your reasonable fear,
what's true in me admits it.
(Though deeper, oh
older than any reason.)
Yes, I could
drown you, you
could foul my depths, it's not
unheard of. What's fish
in me could make flesh of you,
my wet weeds against your thigh, it
could turn nasty.

I could have you
gulping fistfuls fighting yourself
back from me.

I get darker and darker, suck harder.
On-the-brink man, you
wish I'd flash and dazzle again.
You'd make a fetish of zazzing dragonflies?
You want I should zip myself up
with the kingfisher's flightpath, be beautiful?
I say no tricks. I say just trust,
I'll soak through your skin and
slake your thirst.

I watch. You clench,
clench and come into me.

Dreaming Frankenstein

for Lys Hansen, Jacki Parry and June Redfern

She said she
woke up with him in
her head, in her bed.
Her mother-tongue clung to her mouth's roof
in terror, dumbing her, and he came with a name
that was none of her making.

No maidservant ever
in her narrow attic, combing
out her hair in the midnight mirror
on Hallowe'en (having eaten
that egg with its yolk hollowed out
then filled with salt
as a spell to summon up her lover)
– oh never one had such success as this
she had not courted.
The amazed flesh of her
neck and shoulders nettled
at his apparition.

Later, stark staring awake to everything
(the room, the dark parquet, the white high Alps beyond)
all normal in the moonlight
and him gone, save a ton-weight sensation,
the marks fading visibly where
his buttons had bit into her and
the rough serge of his suiting had chafed her sex,
she knew – oh that was not how –
but he'd entered her utterly.

This was the penetration
of seven swallowed apple pips.
Or else he'd slipped like a silver dagger
between her ribs and healed her up secretly
again. Anyway

he was inside her
and getting him out again
would be agony fit to quarter her,
unstitching everything.

Eyes on those high peaks
in the reasonable sun of the morning,
Mary Shelley dressed in damped muslin
and sat down to quill and ink
and icy paper.

Smirnoff for Karloff

for Marilyn Bowering and Bessie Smith

So you're who's been sleeping
in my bed. Well, hello there.
Long time no see.
So you're my Big Fat Little Secret
stretched out cold,
just between you and me.

Between you and me and the bedpost
it's getting a little crowded in here.
Roll over, let me whisper sweet zeroes
in your Good Ear.
Open up your Glad Eye.
Oh my! I'm going to make you.
Going to make you sit up.
Going to make you.
Going to take you to bits.
Going to take you to the cleaners.
Going to make you look cute,
going to let you roly-pole all over me
in your funeral suit –
the one you wear to weddings. Yeah.
With the too short drainpipe trousers
with the brothelcreeper boots with the
tyre-track soles
and the squirt-in-the-eye trick carnation
in your button-hole.

You know Matron
take more than hospital corners to keep
a good man down, oh
yeah. Everything
in applepie order.
All present
and correct. Shipshape. Aye-aye.

He got all my wits around him
his extrasensory senses and his
five straight limbs.
Yes sir,
you'll be up and about again
in no time.

What wouldn't you
give to love me. An arm, and a leg?
Going to make you.
make you sit up,
sit up and beg. Hey, Mister,
Mister can your dog do tricks?
Going to make you,
going to put you to the test,
make you give your all six
nights per week and on Sundays
going to take the rest.

Sure, you can smoke in bed.
It's a free country.
Let me pour you a stiff drink.
You're shivering.
Well, you know what they say, if you
can't take the cold then get outa
the icebox. What's that?
Smirnoff?
Well, you know, Mr Karloff,
I used to think an aphrodisiac was some
kinda confused Tibetan mountain goat
with a freak-out hair-do until I
met my monster and my monster
met his maker.
Oh yeah.

That who been sleeping in my bed.
Same old surprise. Oh goody.
Long time no see.
Ain't going to let nothing come between
my monster and me.

Fetch on the First of January

Nae time eftir the Bells, and the
New Year new in wi the
usual crowd, wi whisky, cheers and kisses –
Ah'd aboot managed the windaes shut
some clown had thrown wide
hopin tae hear the hooters on the Clyde
when the door went.
                        Well, well,
who'd've though Ah'd be staunin there
tae first foot masel?

This some kinnuffa Huntigowk for Hogmany?
Hell-mend-ye, ye're
a bad penny, Jimmy –
Mister Ne'erdy Ne'er-do-Weel
sae chitterin ill-clad for the caul
sae drawn an pale,
oh, wi the black bun burnin a hole
in yir poackit an the coal
a Live Coal.

'Gawn, get' – Ah should shout it,
should shake a stick or ma fist,
oh, but Ah should hunt ye, by Christ,
they wey you chased that big black tyke
that dogged ye wance, mind? –
aw the wey fae Hope Street hame.

Ah'll no let ye near me,
don't make me laugh,
got a much better
Better Half.
Och, aye tae glower at each other
was tae keek in a gey distortin mirror,
yet ye've the neck to come back again
wi yir bare face, Jake Fetch,
the image o my ain.

Ice roon yir mooth when ye kiss me
the cauld plumes o yir breath
Ah'm lukkin daggers
You're lukkin like Death.
Ah'm damned if ye'll get past ma door,
nae fear!

Come away in, stranger, Happy New Year.

Mirror's Song

for Sally Potter

Smash me looking-glass glass
coffin, the one
that keeps your best black self on ice.
Smash me, she'll smash back –
without you she can't lift a finger.
Smash me she'll whirl out like Kali,
trashing the alligator mantrap handbags
with her righteous karate.
The ashcan for the stubbed lipsticks
and the lipsticked butts,
the wet lettuce of fivers!
She'll spill the Kleenex blossoms,
the tissues of lies, the matted
nests of hair from the brushes'
hedgehog spikes, she'll junk
the dead mice and the tampons
the twinkling single eyes
of winkled out diamante, the hatpins,
the whalebone and lycra,
the appleblossom and the underwires,
the chafing iron that kept them maiden,
the Valium and initialled hankies,
the lovepulps and the Librium,
the permanents and panstick and
Coty and Tangee Indelible,
Thalidomide and junk jewellery.

Smash me for your daughters and dead
mothers, for the widowed
spinsters of the first and every war
let her
rip up the appointment cards for the
terrible clinics,
the Greenham summonses, that date
they've handed us. Let her rip.

She'll crumple all the
tracts and the adverts, shred
all the wedding dresses, snap
all the spike-heel icicles
in the cave she will claw out of –
a woman giving birth to herself.

Rapunzstiltskin

& just when our maiden had got
good & used to her isolation,
stopped daily expecting to be rescued,
had come to almost love her tower,
along comes This Prince
with absolutely
all the wrong answers.
Of course she had not been brought up to look for
originality or gingerbread
so at first she was quite undaunted
by his tendency to talk in strung-together cliché.
'Just hang on and we'll get you out of there'
he hollered like a fireman in some soap opera
when she confided her plight (the old
hag inside etc. & how trapped she was);
well, it was corny but
he did look sort of gorgeous
axe and all.
So there she was, humming & pulling
all the pins out of her chignon,
throwing him all the usual lifelines
till, soon, he was shimmying in & out
every other day as though
he owned the place, bringing her
the sex manuals & skeins of silk
from which she was meant, eventually,
to weave the means of her own escape.
'All very well & good,' she prompted,
'but when exactly?'
She gave him till
well past the bell on the timeclock.
She mouthed at him, hinted,
she was keener than a TV quizmaster
that he should get it right.
'I'll do everything in my power,' he intoned, *'but
the impossible* (she groaned) *might*

take a little longer.' He grinned.
She pulled her glasses off.
'All the better
to see you with my dear?' he hazarded.
She screamed, cut off her hair.
'Why, you're beautiful?' he guessed tentatively.
'No, No, No!' she
shrieked & stamped her foot so
hard it sank six cubits through the floorboards.
'I love you?' he came up with
as finally she tore herself in two.

Spinster

This is no way to go on.
Get wise. Accept. Be
a spinster of this parish.
My life's in shards.
I will keep fit in leotards.

Go vegetarian. Accept.
Support good causes.
Be frugal, circumspect.
Keep cats. Take tidy fits.
Go to evening classes.
Keep a nest-egg in the bank.
Try Yoga. Cut your losses.
Accept. Admit you're a bit of a crank –

Oh I may be a *bit* of a crank
but still I get by, frugally. Think positive.
I live and let live. Depend
on nobody. Accept.
Go in for self-improvement.
Keep up with trends.
I'll cultivate my conversation.
I'll cultivate my friends.
I'll grow a herbaceous border.
By hook by crook I'll get my house in order.

Bawd

I'll get all dolled up in my gladrags, stay
up till all hours, oh
up to no good.
It'll amaze you, the company I keep –
and I'll keep them at arm's length –
I've hauled my heart in off my sleeve.

I'll let my hair down,
go blonde, be a bombshell, be on the make,
I'll gold-dig, I'll be frankly fake.

I'll paint my face up, paint the town,
have carmine nails, oh
be a fatal dame.
I've bold eyes, kohl sockets.
I'll look daggers, kill.
My lipstick colour's Merry Hell.

I'd frighten the French.
I'll be a torment, haunt men's dreams,
I'll wear my stockings black with seams.

I'll rouge my cleavage, flaunt myself, my heels
will be perilously high, oh
but I won't sway.
I'll shrug everything off the shoulder,
make wisecracks, be witty off the cuff.
Tell blue jokes in mixed company.

I'll be a bad lot.
I've a brass neck.
There is mayhem in my smile.
No one will guess it's not my style.

Song of Solomon

You
smell nice he said
what is it?
Honey? He nuzzled a soap-trace
in the hollow of her collarbone.
The herbs of her hair?
Salt? He licked
a riverbed between her breasts.

(He'd seemed
not unconvinced by the chemical
attar of roses at her armpit. She tried
to relax have absolute faith in
the expensive secretions of teased civet to
trust the musk at her pulse spots
never think of the whiff of
sourmilk from her navel
the curds of cheese between the toes
the dried blood smell of many small wounds
the stink of fish at her crotch.)

No there he was above her apparently
as happy as a hog rooting for truffles.
She caressed him behind the ear
with the garlic of her cooking-thumb.
She banged shut her eyes
and hoped he would not smell her fear.

The Other Woman

The other woman
lies
between us like a bolster.
When I hit out wild she's
insubstantial a
flurry of feathers a mere
sneezing irritant.
When my shaped and hardened words turn
machine-gun
against you she's rock solid
the sandbag you hide behind.

The other woman
lies
when she says she does not want
your guts for her garterbelt.
I send out spies, they say relax
she's a hag she's just a kid
she's not a patch she's nothing to she's
no oil painting.
I'd know her anywhere.
I look for her in department stores, I scan
every cinema-queue.
Sometimes suddenly in some downtown restaurant
I catch her eye
casting crazily around for me.

The other woman
lies
the other side of my very own mirror.
Sweet, when I smile
straight out for you, she
puts a little twist on it, my
right hand never knows what her left is doing.
She's sinister.
She does not mean you well.

The Hickie

I mouth
sorry in the mirror when I see
the mark I must have made just now
loving you.
Easy to say it's alright
adultery
like blasphemy is for believers but
even in our
situation simple etiquette says
love should leave us both unmarked.
You are on loan to me like a library book
and we both know it.
Fine if you love both of us
but neither of us must too much show it.

In my misted mirror
you trace two toothprints
on the skin of your shoulder and sure
you're almost quick enough
to smile out bright and clear for me
as if it was OK.

Friends again, together in this bathroom
we finish washing love away.

Last Supper

She is getting good and ready to renounce
his sweet flesh.
Not just for lent. (For
Ever)
But meanwhile she is assembling the ingredients
for their last treat, the proper
feast (after all
didn't they always
eat together
rather more than rather well?)
So here she is tearing foliage, scrambling
the salad, maybe lighting candles even, anyway
stepping back to admire the effect of
the table she's made (and oh yes now
will have to lie on) the silverware,
the nicely al-
dente vegetables, the cooked goose.
He could be depended on to bring the bottle
plus betrayal with a kiss.

Already she was imagining it done with, this feast, and
exactly
what kind of leftover hash she'd make of it
among friends, when it was just
The Girls, when those three met again.
What very good soup
she could render from the bones,
then something substantial, something extra
tasty if not elegant.

Yes, there they'd be, cackling around the cauldron,
spitting out the gristlier bits
of his giblets;
gnawing on the knucklebone of some
intricate irony;
getting grave and dainty at the
petit-gout mouthfuls of reported speech.

'That's rich!' they'd splutter,
munching the lies, fat and sizzling as sausages.
Then they'd sink back
gorged on truth
and their own savage integrity,
sleek on it all, preening
like corbies, their bright eyes blinking
satisfied
till somebody would get hungry
and go hunting again.

Everybody's Mother

Of course everybody's mother always and
so on . . .

Always never
loved you enough
or too smothering much.

Of course you were the Only One, your
mother
a machine
that shat out siblings, listen

everybody's mother
was the original Frigid-
aire Icequeen clunking out
the hardstuff in nuggets, mirror-
silvers and ice-splinters that'd stick
in your heart.

Absolutely everyone's mother
was artistic when she was young.

Everyone's mother
was a perfumed presence with pearls, remote
white shoulders when she
bent over in her ball dress
to kiss you in your crib.

Everybody's mother slept with the butcher
for sausages to stuff you with.

Everyone's mother
mythologised herself. You got mixed up
between dragon's teeth and blackmarket stockings.

Naturally
she failed to give you

Positive Feelings
about your own sorry
sprouting body (it was a bloody shame)

but she did
sit up all night sewing sequins
on your carnival costume

so you would have a good time

and she spat
on the corner of her hanky and scraped
at your mouth with sour lace till you squirmed

so you would look smart

And where
was your father all this time?
Away
at the war, or
in his office, or any-
way conspicuous for his
Absence, so

what if your mother did
float around above you
big as a barrage balloon
blocking out the light?

Nobody's mother can't not never do nothing right.

The Man in the Comic Strip

For the man in the comic strip
things are not funny. No wonder he's
running in whichever direction his pisspoor
piston legs are facing
getting nowhere fast.

If only he had the sense he was born with
he'd know there is a world of difference
between the thinks bubble and the speech balloon
and when to keep it zipped, so, with a visible fastener –
But his mouth is always getting him into trouble.
Fistfights blossom round him,
there are flowers explode when the punches connect.
A good idea is a lightbulb, but too seldom.
When he curses, spirals
and asterisks and exclamation marks
whizz around his head like his always palpable distress.
Fear comes off him like petals from a daisy.
Anger brings lightning down on his head and
has him hopping.
Hunger fills the space around him
with floating ideograms of roasted chickens
and iced buns like maidens' breasts the way
the scent of money fills his eyes with dollar signs.

For him the heart is always a beating heart,
True Love –
always comically unrequited.
The unmistakeable silhouette of his one-and-only
will always be kissing another
behind the shades at her window
and, down-at-the-mouth, he'll
always have to watch it from the graphic
lamplit street.

He never knows what is around the corner
although we can see it coming.
When he is shocked his hair stands perfectly on end

but his scream is a total zero and he knows it.
Knows to beware of the zigzags of danger,
knows how very different from
the beeline of zees that is a hostile horizontal buzzing
of singleminded insects swarming after him
are the gorgeous big haphazard zeds of sleep.

Ira and George

for Michael Marra

'First the phonecall'
as the man said – and he sure said a mouthful –
to that 'which comes first, words or music?' question.
Who knows? Except: for every good one
there are ten in the trash, songs you slaved over
that just won't sing, in which no lover ever
will hear some wisecrack twist itself to tell
his unique heartbreak (so sore, so personal) so well
he can't stop humming it. The simplest three-chord melody
                                         might have legs
once it's got the lyric, not tunesmith's ham-and-eggs.
Each catchphrase, colloquialism, each cliché
each snatch of overheard-on-the-subway or street can say
so much, so much when rhymed right, when phrased just-so to fit
its own tune that was born for it.

A Manhattan night in twenty-nine or thirty.
It's late, you're reading Herrick. Just back from a party,
your brother calls out 'Hey let's work!' You watch him shuck
his jacket, loose his black-tie and grab your book.
'Gather ye rosebuds' he says, and slams it shut. He's right.
Hard against the deadline and at night –
shoes off, moon up (just daring you), piano open –
that's when you two can make it happen.
The tune that smells like an onion? Play it very
slow, then *the one that sounds like the Staten Island Ferry*
till you hear the words – brother, they're already there
under the siren and the train and the cab horn blare
of his jazz of endless possibilities that will only fit
its own fine-tuned lyric that is born for it.

Visit, Sonnet

Apprehensive, the poem goes to prison.
Is photographed, has its bag searched, a form to fill,
Checks in money, mobile, rheumatism pills,
Has to declare itself and state its reason.
Brute clang of steel doors, bars, barbed wire, fear
Of what they did or didn't do – and that's none
Of the poem's business. Time that must be *done*,
Not lived, *tholed*, scratched off on walls. A love poem? Here?

We could just stey in oor cells, mind. This is oor choice.
Among the din of D Hall, eight men in jail uniform able
To sit down and face nothing-but-the-poem around this table.
Gey tremulous to start, it soon will find its voice
And in all innocence, all ears, these men will bless
This grateful love poem with their openness.

The Baker

I am as lucky for a funeral
As a sweep is at a wedding
When with his red eyes, furred brush and burnt smell
He blesses bridal lace with his soil and smirching.

Thus do my work-night whites,
The cracks on my dusted boots,
My overall trousers of flour-stiffened linen
Handsel your black ties and pressed mourning suits

Although I am not by your side, nor
Does anyone photograph my – or that rawest – absence.
Dawn delivery to this hotel had me
Shoulder those boards of my generous dozens

As all week neighbours came with bakestuffs
Up the saddest path to your door
Wanting to bring something sweet and light
To where nothing can be so any more.

And now I sleep on sacks washed soft
While you – your time at the cold grave over,
Or after that stare at the core of the terrible oven –
Take tea and funeral cakes together.

Let sober girls in black and white replenish plates
And freshen up the cooling cups with warm
As if tomorrow like live yeast could rise and prove.
I say: such crumbs do no harm.

In nights while I will work and you will grieve
Weak tea, sudden hunger for the heel of a new loaf,
White dawn and the surprise of appetite
Will have you tear a lump of goodness off.

Sooner, later a new season's wind will lift –
Though it may be many daily loaves from this dark hour –
As you let go, fling, and feel the ashes sift
Around your footsteps like spilt flour.

The New-married Miner

My shift is over that was night time all day long.
My love, it's lowsan time. Alone among
these dog-tired colliers my drouth's for home.
Bank up the fire with small coal till I come
and before tomorrow I'll not think again
how sore and small the space I have to hunker in
or how huge and hard but true it pulls all day
as at the pithead, black against the sky,
the big wheel turns. Now my bike's
coggling front wheel clicks and squeaks,
my cold bones ache as hard for home I pedal
still blacked up like a darky minstrel.

My long path home is starved of light
so I must do without.
No moon tonight, so round and white –
its Davy Lamp's gone out.
Frost edges every blackened leaf,
black snot-flowers on my handkerchief.

Heat my bath scalding
and, bonny lass, I'll make
the white lace of the lather black.
Squeeze the hot soapy flannel
at the nape of my neck
and scribble long white chalkmarks down my back.
Put the dark fire to the poker
till the hot flames burst in flower.

Stretch out the towel and I'll stand up.
Hold and fold me
rub and scrub me as hard as you can
till in your white warm arms I'll end up
a pink and naked man, my love
                your pink and naked man.

Poets Need Not

Poets need not be garlanded;
the poet's head
should be innocent of the leaves of the sweet bay tree,
twisted. All honour goes to poetry.

And poets need no laurels. Why be lauded
for the love of trying to nail the disembodied
image with that one plain word to make it palpable,
for listening in to silence for the rhythm capable
of carrying the thought that's not thought yet?
The pursuit's its own reward. So you have to let
the poem come to voice by footering
late in the dark at home, by muttering
syllables of scribbled lines – or what might
be lines, eventually, if you can get it right.

And this, perhaps, in public? The daytime train,
the biro, the back of an envelope, and again
the fun of the wild goose chase
that goes beyond all this fuss.

Inspiration? Bell rings, penny drops,
the light-bulb goes on and tops
the not-good-enough idea that went before?
No, that's not how it goes. You write, you score
it out, you write it in again the same
but somehow with a different stress. This is a game
you very seldom win
and most of your efforts end up in the bin.

There's one hunched and gloomy heron
haunts that nearby stretch of River Kelvin
and it wouldn't if there were no fish.
If it never in all that greyness passing caught a flash,
a gleam of something, made that quick stab.
That's how a poem is after a long nothingness, you grab
at that anything and this is food to you.
It comes through, as leaves do.

All praise to poetry, the way it has
of attaching itself to a familiar phrase
in a new way, insisting it be heard and seen.
Poets need no laurels, surely?
Their poems, when they can make them happen – even rarely –
crown them with green.

Notes on sources

'For my Grandmother Knitting', 'The Choosing', 'After a Warrant Sale', 'Fragmentary', 'Obituary', 'Poem for Other Poor Fools', 'Inventory', 'Revelation', 'Poem for my Sister' and 'Notes on the Inadequacy of a Sketch' were previously published in *Memo for Spring*, Reprographia, 1972 and republished in *Dreaming Frankenstein and Collected Poems 1967–1984*, Polygon, 1984.

'Laundrette' and 'The Bargain' were previously published in *Islands*, Glasgow Print Studio, 1978 and republished in *Dreaming Frankenstein and Collected Poems 1967–1984*, Polygon, 1984.

'My Mother's Suitors', 'Poppies', 'My Rival's House', 'Midsummer Night', 'Rapunzstiltskin', 'Spinster', 'Bawd', 'Song of Solomon', 'The Other Woman', 'The Hickie', 'Last Supper' and 'Everybody's Mother' were previously published in *The Grimm Sisters*, Next Editions in association with Faber and Faber, 1981 and republished in *Dreaming Frankenstein and Collected Poems 1967–1984*, Polygon, 1984.

'In the Dreamschool', 'The Teachers', 'The Offering', 'An Abortion', 'Hafiz on Danforth Avenue', 'Fourth of July Fireworks', 'Ontario October Going West', 'The Empty Song', 'Noises in the Dark', 'What the Pool Said, on Midsummer's Day', 'Dreaming Frankenstein', 'Smirnoff for Karloff', 'Fetch on the First of January' and 'Mirror's Song' were previously published in *Dreaming Frankenstein and Collected Poems 1967–1984*, Polygon, 1984.

'Neckties', 'View of Scotland/Love Poem', 'After the War' and '5th April 1990' were previously published in *Bagpipe Muzak*, Penguin, 1991 and republished in *The Colour of Black and White: Poems 1984–2003*, Polygon, 2003.

'1953', 'Sorting Through' and 'Kidspoem/Bairnsang' were previously published in *Penguin Modern Poets 4*, Penguin, 1995 and republished in *The Colour of Black and White: Poems 1984–2003*, Polygon, 2003.

'A Night In', 'Epithalamium', 'Social History', 'Lanarkshire Girls', 'The Man in the Comic Strip', 'Ira and George', 'The Baker' and 'The New-married Miner' were previously published in *The Colour of Black and White: Poems 1984–2003*, Polygon, 2003.

'Some Old Photographs' was previously published in *New Poems Chiefly in the Scottish Dialect*, Polygon, 2009.

'Poets Need Not' was previously published in *The Times*, 20 January 2011.

'Persimmons' and 'Vow: The Simplest, Hardest and the Truest Thing' were previously pubished in the *Guardian*.

'Visit/Sonnet' was first published in *The Poem Goes To Prison*, an anthology chosen by prisoners in Barlinnie.